JARROLD SHORT WALKS
leisure walks for all ages

South Devon

D1387410

Compiled by
Brian Conduit

JARROLD
publishing

Mapping
sourced from

Ordnance
Survey

Acknowledgements

My thanks for the valuable advice and numerous useful leaflets that I obtained from Devon County Council and the various tourist information centres throughout the area.

Text:	Brian Conduit
Photography:	Brian Conduit
Editor:	Crawford Gillan
Designer:	Sarah Crouch

© Jarrold Publishing 2004

While every care has been taken to ensure the accuracy of the route directions, the publishers cannot accept responsibility for errors or omissions, or for changes in details given. The countryside is not static: hedges and fences can be removed, field boundaries can be altered, footpaths can be rerouted and changes in ownership can result in the closure or diversion of some concessionary paths. Also, paths that are easy and pleasant for walking in fine conditions may become slippery, muddy and difficult in wet weather, while stepping-stones across rivers and streams may become impassable.

If you find an inaccuracy in either the text or maps, please write or e-mail to Jarrold Publishing at the addresses below.

First published 2004
by Jarrold Publishing

Printed in Belgium
by Proost NV, Turnhout. 1/04

Jarrold Publishing
Pathfinder Guides, Whitefriars, Norwich NR3 1JR
E-mail: info@totalwalking.co.uk
www.totalwalking.co.uk

Front cover: Dittisham
Previous page: Hope Cove

Contents

Keymap

SCALE 1:384 615 or 1 INCH to about 6 MILES *1CM to 3.8KM*

0   2   4   6   8   10 KILOMETRES   15

0   2   4   6 MILES 8   10

KEYMAP HEIGHTS SHOWN IN FEET

Introduction

South Devon is justifiably a highly popular walking and holiday destination. It combines a mild climate and rugged coastline with superb beaches, rolling and unspoilt countryside, beautiful river valleys, delightful old towns and picturesque villages. What more could walkers wish for, especially as along the way there are thatched pubs dispensing pasties and cider and old tea shops tempting you with clotted cream teas, just rewards for a vigorous walk.

And let us face it, some of these walks – although short – are quite vigorous. South Devon's terrain is hilly and it is difficult to find a reasonably flat walk of any length. In the following selection of 20 walks only four – Walks 1, 2, 5 and 18 – could be classified as flat. But the rolling hills, deep valleys, steep cliffs and dramatic coastline are the very reasons why walking in South Devon is such a pleasurable experience in any season of the year.

Fairlynch Museum, Budleigh Salterton

Exe valley, near Bickleigh

For the purposes of this guide, South Devon is defined as the area roughly between the southern fringes of Dartmoor – and farther east the M5 motorway – and the sea. It can be divided into three main areas, defined by the numerous rivers which flow roughly north-south across it from the upland wilderness of Dartmoor. Moving from west to east, the first area is the South Hams, extending approximately between Plymouth and the River Dart. Next comes the area between the Dart and the Exe. This is Devon's main holiday area with a string of popular resorts that include Torquay, Paignton, Brixham, Teignmouth and Dawlish. East of the Exe and stretching to the Dorset border is East Devon. Here are more resorts – Exmouth, Budleigh Salterton, Sidmouth, Seaton and Beer – and another superb coastline.

South Hams

The South Hams is southernmost Devon, an almost triangular wedge of land which thrusts southwards into the English Channel. It is characterised by rolling well-wooded hills and deep river valleys which broaden out into long and winding estuaries. These estuaries – Plym, Erme, Avon, Salcombe and Dart – are its chief physical feature. Stretching westwards from the Dart estuary is a rugged and majestic coastline, with steep cliffs overlooking sandy beaches, which offers some of the finest coastal walking in Britain.

This is thinly-populated country. Kingsbridge, at the head of the Salcombe estuary, is the chief town and is a relatively small – if bustling – place. Nearby are delightful villages, many of which have fine churches. Despite the magnetic attraction of the coast, the hills and many river valleys of the South Hams should not be ignored. There is much pleasant walking here, providing variety and a contrast with the coastal routes.

Between Dart and Exe

This area contains Devon's main holiday coast around Tor Bay. The borough of Torbay – simply an administrative convenience – comprises the three main towns of Torquay, Paignton and Brixham, all of which are popular but in different ways. Torquay retains some fine Regency architecture and originally developed in the early 19th century as an aristocratic resort. Paignton, with its excellent sands, was always more of a family resort and the narrow streets and picturesque harbour of the old fishing port of Brixham, nestling below Berry Head, has always attracted thousands of visitors.

Thatcher Point and Rock

Because Torbay is built-up do not think that this is a chiefly urban coastline. Apart from the main seafronts, developments are mainly discreet and unobtrusive and there are well-wooded and totally unspoilt stretches of the South West Way with little walking on tarmac, as revealed by Walk 15.

East of Torbay, the Coast Path continues to Shaldon and the broad Teign estuary, then through the resort of Teignmouth and along more sandstone cliffs to Dawlish at the mouth of the Exe.

Bowling Green marshes, Topsham

East Devon

The coast between the Exe estuary and the Dorset border has been declared a World Heritage Site because of its magnificent expanse of sandstone cliffs. Here the resorts – Exmouth, Budleigh Salterton, Sidmouth, Seaton, Beer – are smaller, quieter and generally more genteel. East of Beer the sandstone changes to chalk, a striking contrast which heralds the start of the Dorset coast.

Away from the excellent and often energetic walking along the coast, there are delightful inland routes in the Otter and Sid valleys and East Devon even has its own mini-Dartmoor, the gorse, tree and heather clad expanses of Woodbury Common. This surprisingly wild area is criss-crossed by paths and tracks and, because of its elevated position, gives fine views over the coast.

Exeter

Exeter has always been the main town and chief focal point of South Devon. Originally founded by the Romans – some of whose walls still survive – it developed into the administrative, military and religious capital of the area. In the late 11th century the Normans began the building of both the cathedral and castle and in the Middle Ages and later, the city became an important wool-exporting port. The first ship canal in England was constructed in Elizabethan times to prolong its maritime life.

Nowadays the old refurbished quayside is one of many historic attractions and, despite extensive wartime damage, Exeter is a rewarding and fascinating city to explore.

Teign Estuary

Ayrmer Cove

Walking in the area

The main attraction for walkers in South Devon is obviously the magnificent coast, traversed throughout by the well-waymarked and well-maintained South West Way, and many of the finest stretches of this coast are featured in the selection of routes. *One word of caution is to take care when venturing onto the cliff tops and exposed headlands in strong winds, especially winter gales. What can seem a benign ramble on a calm summer day can be a rather more hazardous proposition on a blustery day in January and on such days, it is better to switch to a more sheltered inland walk.*

Inland, the paths are generally less frequently used and this means that, as well as getting muddy after wet weather, they may become overgrown during the summer. Neither of these are major problems.

At any time of the year, once away from the main resorts and popular beaches, whether striding along the Coast Path or on inland routes, you will find exhilaration, solitude and a true feel of remoteness.

1 *Stover Lake*

This short, easy and relaxing walk takes you through the attractive woodlands and around the shores of the lake at Stover Country Park. The park was part of the former estate of the Templer family and comprises around 114 acres (46ha) of woodland, lake, marsh and heathland.

START Stover Country Park

DISTANCE 1 ½ miles (2.4km)

TIME 1 hour

PARKING Stover Country Park

ROUTE FEATURES Flat and easy walking through woodland and around a lake

Stover Lake

Begin in front of the Nature Interpretation Centre and take the path to the left of it, signposted To Templer Way, through woodland to a T-junction. Turn left, turn right at a sign to The Pinetum and turn right again at a T-junction. The path bends right between water both sides and at a T-junction in front of the lake, turn left onto the Newton Abbot to Bovey Tracey Cycle Route. Cross a bridge over a stream, turn left along a path and the path bends right and continues in a straight line, keeping more or less parallel with electricity pylons.

PUBLIC TRANSPORT Buses from Newton Abbot and Bovey Tracey

REFRESHMENTS None

PUBLIC TOILETS At start

ORDNANCE SURVEY MAPS Explorer 110 (Torquay & Dawlish), Landranger 191 (Okehampton & North Dartmoor)

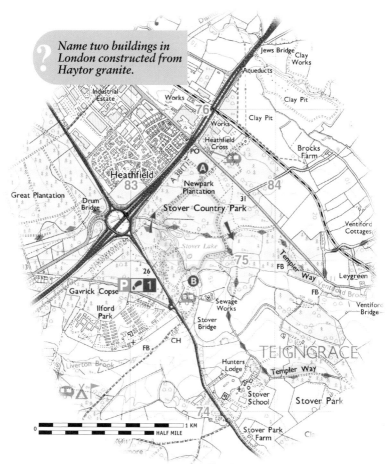

? Name two buildings in London constructed from Haytor granite.

Ⓐ At a crossways, turn right along a path which brings you to Stover Lake. The remainder of the walk is a circuit of this most attractive stretch of water. Keep ahead over a bridge, continue beside the lake, following its curve to the right, and bear right across a boardwalk to a T-junction.

Stover Country Park is situated between Newton Abbot and Bovey Tracey. Its main feature, the 10-acre (4ha) lake, has been designated as a **Site of Special Scientific Interest** and is particularly important for dragonflies and its abundance of wildfowl. A new Nature Interpretation, opened in 2000, has displays illustrating the wealth of animal and plant life in the park.

Looking across to Stover Lake

B Turn right along a tree-lined path and turn left at another T-junction. At the next T-junction, turn left again to return to the start. ●

By the lakeside

The history of **Stover** is basically the story of the rise of the Templer family. It began with James Templer, a poor orphan in Exeter, who ran away to sea as a young man and made a fortune in India. On his return to England, he bought a large, rundown estate on the southern edge of Dartmoor in 1765 and began the building of **Stover House**, now a school, and the landscaping of the grounds. In 1792 his son – also called James – built the **Stover Canal** to carry clay from workings on the estate to the River Teign for export from Teignmouth. Later in 1820 his grandson, George Templer, constructed a tramway to bring granite from his quarries on Dartmoor to link up with the canal. By about 1850 the granite quarries had become uneconomic but clay continued to be transported along the canal until the 1950s.

Topsham and the Exe Estuary

START Topsham, Quayside
DISTANCE 2 miles (3.2km)
TIME 1 hour
PARKING Topsham
ROUTE FEATURES Flat and easy walking along roads and tarmac paths

Although a predominantly urban walk, close to the town and entirely on roads and tarmac paths, it does have a rural feel and there are fine and wide views across the marshes and mudflats of the Exe estuary to the Haldon Hills on the other side. Topsham is a fascinating and most attractive little town, well worth a thorough exploration.

Start at the Quay by the Steam Packet and Lighter inns and facing the river, turn left along the Strand. Where the road ends, keep ahead along a tarmac path – this is the Goat Walk – on an embankment raised above the marshes and mudflats of the Exe estuary. The path bends left to emerge onto a lane (Bowling Green Road).

Ⓐ Keep ahead and just after the lane bends left, a gate on the right leads to a RSPB Nature Reserve viewing platform, from which there are fine views of the estuary,

Attractive Topsham

PUBLIC TRANSPORT Buses and trains from Exeter and Exmouth
REFRESHMENTS Pubs and cafés at Topsham
PUBLIC TOILETS Topsham
ORDNANCE SURVEY MAPS Explorer 114 (Exeter & the Exe Valley) or 110 (Torquay & Dawlish), Landranger 192 (Exeter & Sidmouth)

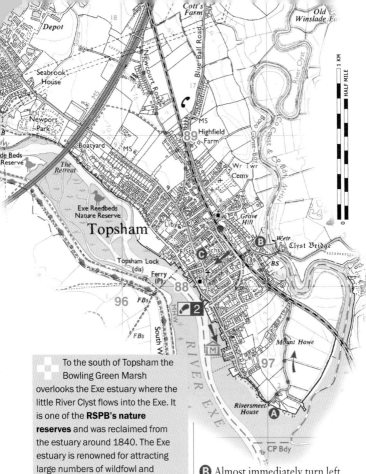

To the south of Topsham the Bowling Green Marsh overlooks the Exe estuary where the little River Clyst flows into the Exe. It is one of the **RSPB's nature reserves** and was reclaimed from the estuary around 1840. The Exe estuary is renowned for attracting large numbers of wildfowl and wading birds.

Bowling Green Marsh and the confluence of the Exe and the Clyst. Continue along the lane which curves left beside a railway embankment and bears right – now called Elm Grove Road – to cross a railway bridge. Keep ahead to join a main road and bear left.

B Almost immediately turn left along an enclosed path. Go through a kissing-gate, cross the railway line, turn left to go through a gate onto a road and turn right. At a footpath sign to Town Centre, turn left along an enclosed tarmac track which becomes a road. Where it bends right, keep ahead to emerge into Fore Street opposite Topsham church and turn right.

C Take the first street on the left (Exe Street), signposted to River and Ferry. At a T-junction, turn left along a narrow street beside the estuary, passing below the church, and follow it back to the start. ●

As you walk along the Goat Walk, which seaside resort can be seen ahead at the mouth of the estuary?

Topsham – just downstream from Exeter – was an important port in the Middle Ages and later, mainly involved in the exporting of wool. It remains a delightfully unspoilt small town with a wealth of old buildings and is particularly noted for its large number of 17th and 18th century houses, many built in the Dutch style. Some of these can be seen on the first part of the walk along the Strand and one of the finest of them now houses the **Topsham Museum**.

The Exe estuary at Topsham

3 *Historic Exeter*

START Exeter, the Guildhall

DISTANCE 2¼ miles (3.6km)

TIME 1½ hours

PARKING Exeter

ROUTE FEATURES Historic town walk entirely on tarmac paths

Substantial stretches remain of Exeter's Roman and medieval walls and the walk mainly follows their course as it takes you on a tour of the ancient city, passing most of its historic attractions. These include the Guildhall, the magnificent Gothic cathedral, Norman castle, medieval priory and the attractive restored quayside. There are plenty of detailed information boards along the way.

Start by the fine 14th-century Guildhall and with your back to it, turn left along High Street. Turn right along Martins Lane (signposted to Cathedral), passing the Old Ship Inn and St Martin's church, into the Cathedral Close. Keep ahead, passing Mol's Coffee House, once a meeting place for Elizabethan sea captains, go through a gap in the walls and turn left along Southernhay West. At a T-junction, turn left to return to High Street and turn left again. Turn right into Castle Street and walk up to the gatehouse of Rougemont Castle.

Customs House, Exeter

PUBLIC TRANSPORT Exeter is served by buses and trains from all the surrounding towns

REFRESHMENTS Pubs and cafés in Exeter

PUBLIC TOILETS Exeter

ORDNANCE SURVEY MAPS Explorer 114 (Exeter & the Exe Valley), Landranger 192 (Exeter & Sidmouth)

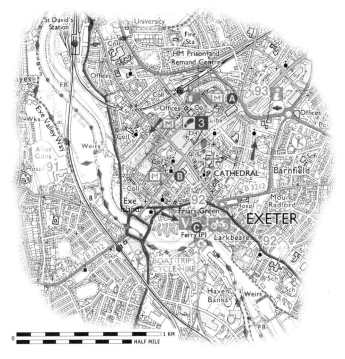

A Turn left into Rougemont Gardens and at a fork, take the right-hand upper path to keep by the castle wall. At the next fork, take the left-hand lower path below Athelstan's Tower and the path curves left by the city walls again. Turn right through an arch in the walls into Northernhay Gardens, turn left, exit the gardens and keep ahead to a crossroads. Continue along Northernhay Street, heading down to a T-junction, turn left along Lower North Street and go up steps to a crossroads. Turn right

Exeter Cathedral is a masterpiece of Gothic architecture. Apart from the twin towers of the original Norman cathedral that rise above the transepts, it was mainly built between 1275 and 1375. The most striking feature of the exterior is the ornate 14th century west front with its screen of statues. Inside it is noted for the fine, uninterrupted vaulting that runs for almost the whole length of the building. The cathedral fortunately survived the bombing in World War II which destroyed so many of the old streets and buildings around it.

Southern Hay, Exeter

along Bartholomew Street East, follow the road to the left and, where it bends right, keep ahead along The Mint. Bend first left and then right to pass to the left of St Nicholas' Priory. The main survival of this Norman priory is a guest wing. Keep ahead to Fore Street.

? *Can you find what is supposed to be the narrowest street in the world near the end of the walk?*

B Turn right and turn left into King Street. Take the first road on the right and descend picturesque Stepcote Hill to the church of St Mary Steps at the bottom of the steps. Keep ahead to cross a dual carriageway, turn left and turn right down steps. Before reaching the bottom – at a signpost 'City Wall Walk and Quay' – continue along a cobbled path beside the wall which joins a cobbled track. Turn right down to the Historic Quayside.

C The route continues up the steps ahead, still by the wall. Turn sharp left up steps to go through a gap in the wall and turn right up more steps – now the wall is on the right – to emerge into a car park. Turn right but before reaching a road, turn right up steps onto the wall, turn left to cross a footbridge over the road and descend steps on the other side. Turn left along South Street, turn right into Palace Gate and the road heads uphill, bending first left and then right, to emerge into the Cathedral Close again. In front of the west front of the cathedral, turn left up steps, keep to the right of a war memorial and keep ahead to High Street. The Guildhall is just to the right. ●

Exeter originated as the Roman town of Isca Dumnoniorum and it was the Romans who began the construction of the walls. These were added to and rebuilt by the Normans, a process which was repeated several times until as late as the 17th century. In the late 11th century, William the Conqueror built **Rougemont Castle** in the north east corner of the walls and throughout the Middle Ages and later the city was a major administrative, military, religious and commercial centre. The construction of a ship canal in the 16th century enhanced its importance as a port, mainly exporting wool, and its quayside became a hive of activity, reaching its heyday in the 18th century. The **Historic Quayside** has been restored as an attractive recreational and leisure area and some of the impressive former warehouses have been converted into pubs, restaurants and coffee shops.

Exeter Cathedral

4 *Start Point*

START Start Point
DISTANCE 2 miles (3.2km)
TIME 1 hour
PARKING Start Point
ROUTE FEATURES Easy walking on the Coast Path around a headland

From the prominent headland of Start Point, there are magnificent and extensive views northwards across the wide sweep of Start Bay and westwards across Lannacombe Bay. The route follows a tarmac path along the north side of the point to the lighthouse at the tip and then continues along the dramatic south side before heading gently uphill across the neck of the headland to the start.

Begin by climbing the stone stile beside a gate at the far end of the car park and walk along an enclosed, gently descending tarmac path to the lighthouse at the tip of Start Point. Retrace your steps to a Coast Path sign.

An information board at the start of the walk points out the sites of the **lost villages of Start Bay**. These are former fishing villages that have been abandoned after being destroyed by the sea. They include Hallsands – just below the point – Slapton Cellars and Strete-Undercliffe.

A Turn left onto a path which heads over the narrow headland and curves right to contour along the south side of Start Point. The path later descends to the base of the cliffs and curves right.

? *What is the name of the organisation responsible for Britain's lighthouses?*

B At a fingerpost above the lovely cove of Great Mattiscombe Sand – where the Coast Path bends left – keep ahead to a gate. Go through, head gently uphill along an enclosed path, going through two more gates, and after the second one, turn left over a stone stile to the start.

PUBLIC TRANSPORT None
REFRESHMENTS None
PUBLIC TOILETS None
ORDNANCE SURVEY MAPS Explorer OL20 (South Devon), Landranger 202 (Torbay & South Dartmoor)

Start Point

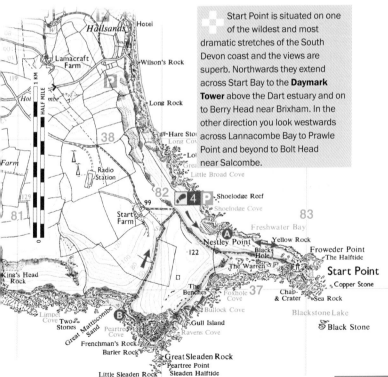

Start Point is situated on one of the wildest and most dramatic stretches of the South Devon coast and the views are superb. Northwards they extend across Start Bay to the **Daymark Tower** above the Dart estuary and on to Berry Head near Brixham. In the other direction you look westwards across Lannacombe Bay to Prawle Point and beyond to Bolt Head near Salcombe.

5 Slapton: Nature Reserve and Village

START Slapton Sands, Memorial car park
DISTANCE 2½ miles (4km)
TIME 1½ hours
PARKING Slapton Memorial car park
ROUTE FEATURES Easy walking along paths through a nature reserve and by a lake

Although the walk starts on the coast by Slapton Sands, most of it is through a well-wooded nature reserve beside the lake of Slapton Ley. At about the halfway point, you pass through the quiet, attractive and interesting village of Slapton.

Turn right out of the car park, passing the memorial, and turn left along the lane signposted to Slapton. After crossing Slapton Bridge, turn left through a kissing-gate, at a public footpath sign to Deer Bridge via Nature Trail, to enter the nature reserve. Follow an undulating path through trees either above or beside Slapton Ley – there are a series of gates and stiles and steps and boardwalks in places – eventually bending right away from the lake and continuing through woodland to a fingerpost and stile.

The memorial at Slapton Sands

PUBLIC TRANSPORT Buses from Dartmouth, Kingsbridge and Plymouth
REFRESHMENTS Pubs at Slapton
PUBLIC TOILETS At start
ORDNANCE SURVEY MAPS Explorer OL20 (South Devon), Landranger 202 (Torbay & South Dartmoor)

In the tranquil surroundings of Slapton it is difficult to imagine that in the spring of 1944, the village – along with others in the locality – resounded with the noise of tanks and shelling as it was used as a training ground for **American troops** in preparation for the D-Day landings in Normandy. The villagers had to evacuate their homes for about seven months. Some of the buildings were destroyed and it took a long time for conditions to return to normal after the war. There is a fine medieval church and the ruined tower at the side of the Tower Inn is the only surviving remnant of a **College of Priests**, founded in 1373.

A Climb the stile, keep ahead and the path bends left in front of a gate to emerge from the trees and heads gently uphill. Climb a stile onto a tarmac track, continue uphill and go through a gate onto a lane. Turn left, head downhill through the village of Slapton – *a detour along a lane on the right leads to the two pubs, church and ruined tower.*

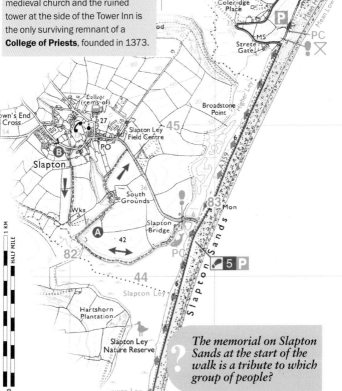

The memorial on Slapton Sands at the start of the walk is a tribute to which group of people?

B Soon after the lane starts to ascend, turn left along a tarmac track, at a public footpath sign to Slapton Ley. Continue along a rough enclosed track – later by a right field edge – and descend gently to a gate. Go through and continue downhill along an enclosed path into the nature reserve again to a T-junction. Turn left along a path signed 'Permissive Path to Nature Reserve' and the route continues across a boardwalk and up steps to a T-junction. Turn right, **A** here rejoining the outward route, and retrace your steps beside Slapton Ley to the start.

Slapton Ley was originally a bay of the sea but is now cut off from it by a long ridge of shingle. It is the largest natural freshwater lake in the West Country and forms the centrepiece of a **National Nature Reserve**, surrounded by reed bed, marsh, shingle and attractive woodland.

The lake at Slapton Ley

Woodbury Common

START Woodbury Common, Four Firs Cross, junction of B3180 and B3179
DISTANCE 2¾ miles (4.4km)
TIME 1½ hours
PARKING Four Firs Cross car park
ROUTE FEATURES Undulating walking across open heathland and through woodland

The route takes you across part of Woodbury Common, a large and surprisingly wild area of woodland and heath that lies to the north of Exmouth and Budleigh Salterton. It includes the highest point on the common, the tree-covered, prehistoric fort of Woodbury Castle, around 600 ft (183m) high and a superb vantage point over common and coast.

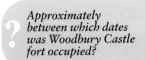 From the car park entrance, cross the lane and take the path opposite – there is a mauve waymark here. The path soon widens into a track and heads gently uphill across the gorse, bracken and heather of the common, keeping roughly parallel with the road on the left, to reach Woodbury Castle car park.

? *Approximately between which dates was Woodbury Castle fort occupied?*

Woodbury Common

PUBLIC TRANSPORT None
REFRESHMENTS None
PUBLIC TOILETS None
ORDNANCE SURVEY MAPS Explorer 115 (Exmouth & Sidmouth), Landranger 192 (Exeter & Sidmouth)

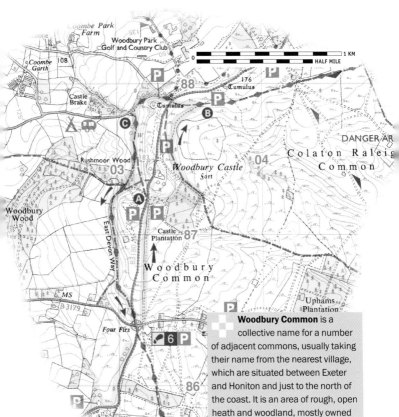

A In the right-hand corner of the car park, take the path to the right of a Clinton Devon Estates information board. The path curves right and continues alongside the earthworks of the fort to a T-junction. Turn left and the path curves right and continues through woodland to emerge onto a track. Turn left along this broad track by the right edge of woodland and at a crossways, turn left again – in the

Woodbury Common is a collective name for a number of adjacent commons, usually taking their name from the nearest village, which are situated between Exeter and Honiton and just to the north of the coast. It is an area of rough, open heath and woodland, mostly owned by the Devon Clinton Estates, criss-crossed by tracks and footpaths and a paradise for walkers who wish for some of the 'wilderness experience' normally only achieved in South Devon by visiting Dartmoor. Numerous car parks make excellent starting points.

direction of a blue waymark – and continue along the right edge of the trees. Follow the winding path to a T-junction. Turn right, continue across the open common and at a fork take the left-hand path.

B About 200 yds (183m) farther on – and about 50 yds (46m) before the next waymarked fork – turn sharp left onto a clear path to the B3180. Cross over and take the lane opposite, passing the entrance to Woodbury Park Hotel, Golf and Country Club.

C After a quarter of a mile (0.4km), turn left, at public bridleway and East Devon Way signs, along a woodland track. Following the East Devon Way signs all the time, continue along the track through trees and across more open common, taking the right hand track at the first fork

Despite its name, **Woodbury Castle** is not a castle but a prehistoric hill fort. Although its extensive earthworks are covered by trees and severed by a road, they can still be traced. The fort stands at the highest point on the common, around 600 ft (183m) above sea level, and is a magnificent viewpoint.

and again at a second fork, and bearing right on joining another track. The track eventually curves left and heads gently uphill to the B3180 again. Cross over and take the path opposite which curves right to a track. Turn right and the car park is just ahead. ●

Wild woodland and heath at Woodbury Common

7 Aveton Gifford and the River Avon

START Aveton Gifford

DISTANCE 2¾ miles (4.4km)

TIME 1½ hours

PARKING Aveton Gifford, Timbers car park by bridge

ROUTE FEATURES Easy walking along lanes and paths by an estuary, through woodland, across fields and through a village

The first part of the route is along a lane by the estuary of the River Avon. You then walk through woodland above a creek and continue across fields to the village of Aveton Gifford. The final stretch is along the attractive village street. Please note that the first part of the walk beside the estuary is along a lane that is sometimes under water for a few hours either side of high tide. Please check with Kingsbridge Tourist Information Centre (Tel: 01548 853195) before setting out.

Turn right out of the car park along a lane beside the Avon estuary. *Take care as this is a narrow lane and it can be busy at times.*

Ⓐ On reaching a ford over a creek, bear right along a path below a wooded cliff which curves right beside the creek. Look out for where a yellow waymark directs you to bear right to climb a stile

The Avon estuary

PUBLIC TRANSPORT Buses from Dartmouth, Kingsbridge and Plymouth

REFRESHMENTS Pub at Aveton Gifford

PUBLIC TOILETS None

ORDNANCE SURVEY MAPS Explorer OL 20 (South Devon), Landranger 202 (Torbay & South Dartmoor)

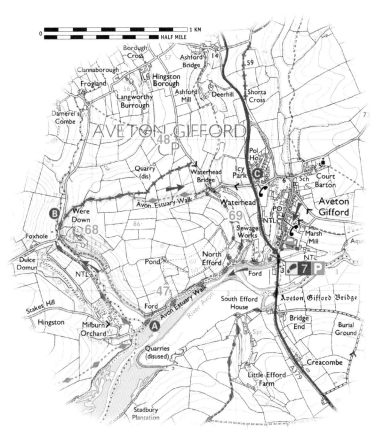

Aveton Gifford comprises little more than one long street (Fore Street) which stretches for about ½ mile (0.8km) from the church to the bridge over the River Avon. The cruciform church has a chunky, fortress-like appearance and its most unusual feature is the circular tower with a conical roof at the south west corner of the central tower. It was built in the 14th century and restored in the 1950s.

and continue through woodland, heading up to a T-junction. Turn left along a path to a lane and turn right.

B At a public byway sign to Drunkards Hill, bear right along an uphill, tree-lined track. The track levels out and on emerging into a small open area, turn right over a stile, bear left and walk

? Why did the church at Aveton Gifford have to be restored after the Second World War?

diagonally across the corner of a field to a stone stile. Climb it, turn right along the right field edge, follow the edge round to the left and at a hedge corner, continue downhill across the field, keeping along the left edge of a group of trees to a stile. Climb it, descend steps to a tarmac track, turn left and in front of a row of cottages, turn sharp right down a narrow lane. The lane bends left and continues uphill to the A379.

C Cross carefully, turn left onto a tarmac path which bends sharply to the right and then turns left to a road. Keep ahead downhill under a canopy of trees to a T-junction and turn right. *At the next T-junction turn left uphill to visit Aveton Gifford church*; otherwise follow the road to the right through the village to the A379 again and cross over by a traffic island to return to the start. ●

The Devonian River Avon – less well-known than its namesakes in other parts of England – rises on Dartmoor and flows southwards across the South Hams into Bigbury Bay. South of Aveton Gifford it becomes tidal. A waymarked route – the Avon Estuary Walk – has been created along both sides of the estuary between Aveton Gifford, Bigbury-on-Sea and Bantham. The **ferry across the river at Bantham** enables it to be converted into a circular walk.

Aveton Gifford church

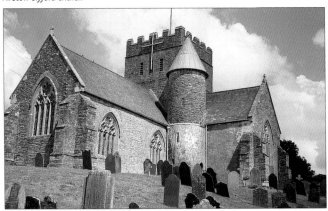

Berry Pomeroy

Field paths, quiet lanes and tracks take you from the small village of Berry Pomeroy to the impressive remains of a castle, in an isolated location amidst woodland. There are fine views over the village and the Dart valley on the return leg.

START Berry Pomeroy

DISTANCE 3 miles (4.8km)

TIME 1½ hours

PARKING Roadside parking at Berry Pomeroy

ROUTE FEATURES Easy walking along lanes, field paths and woodland tracks

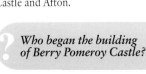 The walk starts at the crossroads in Berry Pomeroy. Turn down the road signposted to Church and where it bends right, turn left, at a public footpath sign, along an enclosed track. Pass between gateposts into a field and head gently uphill across it, veering slightly right away from the left edge and making for a gate in the far left-hand corner. Go through onto a road, turn right but almost immediately bear left along a lane signposted to Berry Pomeroy Castle and Afton.

Berry Pomeroy church

? *Who began the building of Berry Pomeroy Castle?*

PUBLIC TRANSPORT Buses from Torquay, Totnes and Dartmouth

REFRESHMENTS Tearoom at Berry Pomeroy Castle

PUBLIC TOILETS None

ORDNANCE SURVEY MAPS Explorer 110 (Torquay & Dawlish), Landranger 202 (Torbay & South Dartmoor)

Berry Pomeroy Castle has been owned by two families throughout its history, the Pomeroys and later the Seymours. The ruins, which occupy a cliff above a secluded wooded valley about 1 mile (1.6km) from the village and church, comprise two quite distinct parts: a medieval gatehouse and walls and an Elizabethan palace. Originally built in the 12th century, the Seymours decided to modernise it in the late 16th century and began the construction of an elaborate mansion. This was never completed and the castle was abandoned in the late 17th century and subsequently fell into ruin.

Ⓐ After a quarter of a mile (0.4km), turn left at the castle entrance, climb a stile and walk gently downhill along a tarmac drive to the castle. Just before reaching the car park, bear left onto a path which heads downhill through woodland to a tarmac track. Turn right to a T-junction and turn right along a lane.

Ⓑ The lane heads uphill through woodland, levels off and descends to the castle entrance. **Ⓐ** Here you pick up the outward route and retrace your steps to the start. ●

Berry Pomeroy Castle

The village of Berry Pomeroy is little more than a hamlet and lies just to the north east of Totnes with views over the Dart valley. It is dominated by the tall west tower of its **medieval church**. Inside are monuments to the Pomeroy and Seymour families, the occupants of Berry Pomeroy Castle.

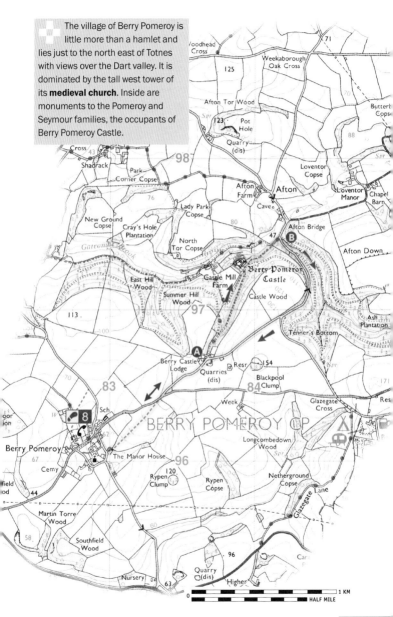

9 *Berry Head and Brixham*

After an opening stretch along the coast above St Mary's Bay, the route heads inland across the neck of the headland and descends into Brixham. A walk beside the harbour is followed by an easy climb back onto Berry Head, passing the Napoleonic forts. There are grand views from the headland across Tor Bay and Start Bay.

START Berry Head Country Park
DISTANCE 3¼ miles (5.2km)
TIME 2 hours
PARKING Berry Head Country Park
ROUTE FEATURES Roads, tracks and coast path, one gentle climb

Brixham harbour

Start by taking the lane to the right of the visitor centre and at a public footpath sign to Coast Path, turn left along an enclosed path to a stile. Climb it, keep by a wall on the left and climb a series of stone stiles as you follow the coast around Durl Head and above St Mary's Bay. Shortly after going through a kissing-gate you reach a fork.

> **How high are the ramparts of the Northern Fort on Berry Head?**

PUBLIC TRANSPORT None to the start but Brixham is served by buses from Torquay, Paignton and Kingswear
REFRESHMENTS Pubs and cafés at Brixham, café at Berry Head North Fort
PUBLIC TOILETS At start, Brixham, Shoalstone Point, North Fort café
ORDNANCE SURVEY MAPS Explorer OL20 (South Devon), Landranger 202 (Torbay & South Dartmoor)

A Take the right-hand enclosed tarmac path to a lane and keep ahead along Centry Road. Turn right at a crossroads, follow the road around a left bend and head down Ranscombe Road to a T-junction in the centre of Brixham.

The two substantial stone forts on Berry Head were built during the **Napoleonic Wars** to protect Torbay, an anchorage for the British fleet, from an expected French invasion. At their height they were home to up to 1000 troops and 50 horses. The Northern Fort is the best preserved and the former guardhouse there is now a café.

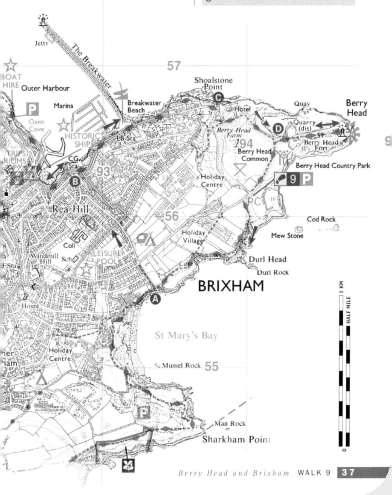

B The main town and harbour are to the left but at the T-junction the route continues to the right along Berry Head Road beside the harbour. After about half a mile (0.8km), turn left along a tarmac path and on reaching Shoalstone car park, turn right through it.

C Turn left along a tarmac drive to Berry Head Country Park, follow it around a right bend and at a Berry Head Country Park sign, turn left through a kissing-gate. Continue through woodland, climb steps and head steadily uphill to emerge onto the open cliff top. Keep ahead – later along a tarmac track – to a T-junction.

D Turn left to enter the Northern Fort and keep ahead to the

lighthouse on the tip of the headland. Retrace your steps to the T-junction and keep ahead, in the Southern Fort and Visitor Centre direction, and the track leads back to the start, passing to the right of the Southern Fort. ●

For generations a boat trip across the bay to **Brixham** has become an essential part of a holiday at the nearby resorts of Torquay and Paignton. It is still a working port and retains the atmosphere of a traditional fishing village, with narrow streets and rows of colourful houses and cottages rising steeply from the harbour. In 1688 Brixham played a major role in British history when **William of Orange** landed here at the start of his successful campaign to win the throne from his father-in-law, **James II**. There is a statue to him by the harbour.

Fort on Berry Head

Dittisham and the River Dart

START Dittisham, The Ham car park

DISTANCE 3¾ miles (5.2km)

TIME 2 hours

PARKING The Ham car park

ROUTE FEATURES Lanes, tracks and field paths, several short climbs

10

The starting point is a beautiful spot adjoining meadows beside the River Dart. From there you head up into the attractive village of Dittisham, walk beside a creek and continue along quiet, narrow lanes. On the final part of the route, which is a steady climb across fields, there are superb views over the winding Dart and the valley to the southern edge of Dartmoor.

Head uphill along the tarmac track to a road and bear left into Dittisham, passing the fine medieval church. At a T-junction in the village centre, turn right, not along the road but down steps. Continue downhill along a lane between thatched cottages. The lane bends left, heads uphill and curves right to the road. Head downhill along the road and keep beside a creek at the bottom.

A At a public footpath sign, turn right over a plank footbridge.

Dart valley near Dittisham

PUBLIC TRANSPORT Occasional buses from Dartmouth and Totnes, ferry (Easter to October) from Dartmouth

REFRESHMENTS Pubs at Dittisham

PUBLIC TOILETS At start

ORDNANCE SURVEY MAPS Explorer OL20 (South Devon), Landranger 202 (Torbay & South Dartmoor)

Dittisham church

The steep, narrow streets of Dittisham lie amid rolling hills on the west bank of the River Dart. Dominating the village is the imposing church, which dates mainly from the early 14th century although the tall west tower is probably older. An unusual feature for a village church is the two-storied south porch.

Cross another footbridge into woodland, cross a track, ascend steps, climb a stile and turn left along the bottom edge of a sloping field. Climb a stile and keep ahead along an attractive, tree-lined path. Climb another stile onto a lane and turn left downhill. After crossing a bridge the lane bends left uphill and you turn right along a lane signposted to Coombe.

B At a sign to Kingston, follow the narrow lane around a left bend. Head uphill, bending left, and then continue downhill to another left bend at the bottom.

Which king of England has his coat of arms above the door inside Dittisham church?

C Just after the left bend, turn right over a half-hidden stile to the right of a gate. Turn left and walk initially along the right field edge, by a hedge on the right. Bear right, head uphill across the field, skirting the end of a hedge on the left, and continue more steeply up to a waymarked post. Bear left, continue – still uphill – by the right edge of the field and over the brow a magnificent view unfolds over the Dart valley, with the uplands of Dartmoor on the horizon. After climbing a stile, head gently down by the right field edge to a kissing-gate, go through and continue down a tree-lined track to a road. Turn right into Dittisham and retrace your steps to the car park.

The winding **Dart** is considered to be one of the most beautiful rivers in England. Formed by the junction of the East Dart and West Dart – both of which rise on Dartmoor – it flows southwards from the moor through the historic town of Totnes. Between Totnes and Dartmouth comes the loveliest part of the valley: the river meanders between steep hillsides and wooded slopes and there are attractive villages close to its banks.

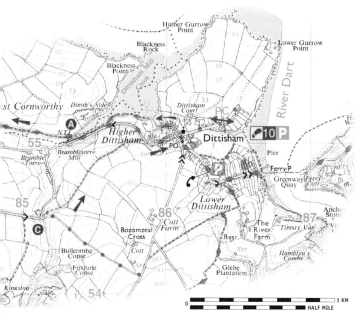

11 *Torcross and Beesands*

START Torcross
DISTANCE 3½ miles (5.6km)
TIME 2 hours
PARKING Torcross
ROUTE FEATURES An undulating and well-wooded route – quite steep in places – with a flat stretch beside the sea

There are superb views over Start Bay and Slapton Ley both at the start and end of the route. In between, there is attractive walking through woodland, you pass through the small, isolated coastal village of Beesands and a relaxing stroll beside the beach precedes the final climb over the wooded headland of Dun Point. This is a fairly energetic walk with two climbs: the first is long – 1 mile (1.6km) – but gradual, the second is shorter but steeper.

Beesands

👣 Turn right out of the car park along the road into the village and where the road bends right, keep ahead along an uphill lane beside the Torcross Tavern. The lane bends right and continues steadily uphill, passing Torcross Viewpoint, from where there is a superb vista over Slapton Ley and Start Bay.

> **?** *On what date was the Sherman tank at the side of the car park recovered from the sea?*

PUBLIC TRANSPORT Buses from Dartmouth, Kingsbridge and Plymouth
REFRESHMENTS Pubs and cafés at Torcross, pub at Beesands
PUBLIC TOILETS Torcross and Beesands
ORDNANCE SURVEY MAPS Explorer OL20 (South Devon), Landranger 202 (Torbay & South Dartmoor)

A After ¾ mile (1.2km) – where a narrow lane comes in from the right – turn left through a kissing-gate, at a public footpath sign to Beeson. Head uphill across a field – later by woodland on the right – go through a kissing-gate in the corner and turn left along a tarmac track. At a fingerpost, turn right (signposted Beeson) along a well-waymarked path through woodland to a stile. Climb it, continue downhill along the left edge of fields and go through a gate in the bottom corner of the last field. Cross a track and, keeping to the left of a farmhouse, walk along an enclosed track to reach two gates. Go through the right-hand gate and continue

Torcross is situated beside the sea at the southern end of the freshwater lake of Slapton Ley. After being recovered from the sea many years after the war, the Sherman tank in the car park was placed here as a memorial to more than 900 American servicemen, killed by a surprise **German attack** in April 1944 while rehearsing for the D-Day landings. News of the tragedy was suppressed at the time and it remained largely unknown until a local man, **Ken Small**, wrote a book about it and played a major role in organising the tank memorial.

along an undulating tree-lined path which widens into a track and emerges onto a lane. Turn left through the hamlet of Beeson.

Tank memorial at Torcross

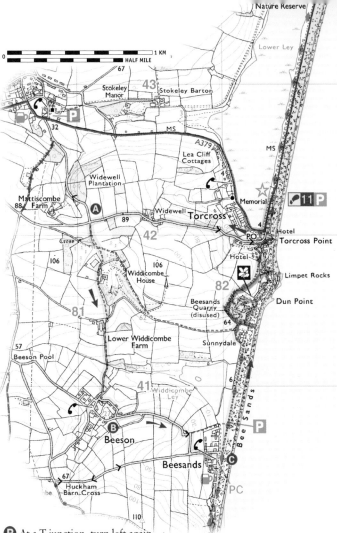

B At a T-junction, turn left again along a lane. From here there are grand views of the coast and Widdicombe Ley. Head downhill, follow the lane around first a left bend and then a right bend and at a T-junction, turn left into Beesands.

C The lane bends right through the village but the route continues to the left along a straight track alongside the beach. For the rest of the walk you follow the regular

Coast Path signs. At a waymarked post, follow the track to the left, passing to the left of a house, and continue uphill along a narrow, enclosed path. The climb through woodland over the headland is quite a steep one and there are steps in places. After going through a gate, head gently downhill along the left edge of a field to another gate, go through that one and continue down an enclosed path. The path – which becomes a tarmac one – bends sharply to the

The remote fishing village of **Beesands** is little more than a line of cottages and a pub beside a flat stretch of coast. It has always been vulnerable to flooding and its latest sea defences were completed in 1993. Just to the north is the lake of **Widdicombe Ley**, a smaller version of Slapton Ley.

right, then sharply left and at a footpath post, turn right along a track. Turn left down steps and at the bottom, keep ahead to return to the start.

Slapton Ley from Torcross

12 *Bickleigh: Mill, Castle and Village*

START Bickleigh Mill

DISTANCE 4 miles (6.4km)

TIME 2 hours

PARKING Bickleigh Mill, not in the Mill or Devon Railway Centre car parks but at the large car park reached by turning right under the road bridge

ROUTE FEATURES Quiet lanes and field and woodland paths, one climb, some overgrown and uneven paths and a wobbly bridge

After an opening walk along a lane, passing the remains of Bickleigh Castle, you continue across fields, crossing a footbridge over the River Exe. Then comes another stretch along a lane, followed by a climb through woodland and across fields. From the higher points there are superb views over the Exe valley. A descent into Bickleigh village leads on to the start. Nervous and less agile walkers, and people with young children, are warned that the crossing of the river can be a daunting prospect; the footbridge is narrow and sways alarmingly.

Turn left out of the car park, go under the road bridge and at a T-junction, turn left to the main road. Keep ahead over Bickleigh Bridge and continue along the A3072 to Crediton, signposted to Bickleigh Castle. At the next sign to Bickleigh Castle, turn left along a shady lane beside the River Exe, passing the gatehouse of Bickleigh Castle. Continue along the lane for another mile (1.6km).

Ⓐ Just after passing the thatched Traymill Farm on the left, turn left through a gate and walk through the farmyard. Go through another gate, head across a rough and uneven field and cross a narrow and wobbly suspension footbridge over the River Exe. Keep ahead to go through a kissing-gate, bear right diagonally across a field, go through a kissing-gate in the corner and immediately turn left through

PUBLIC TRANSPORT Buses from Exeter and Tiverton

REFRESHMENTS Pubs at Bickleigh, café at Bickleigh Mill

PUBLIC TOILETS None

ORDNANCE SURVEY MAPS Explorer 114 (Exeter & the Exe Valley), Landranger 192 (Exeter & Sidmouth)

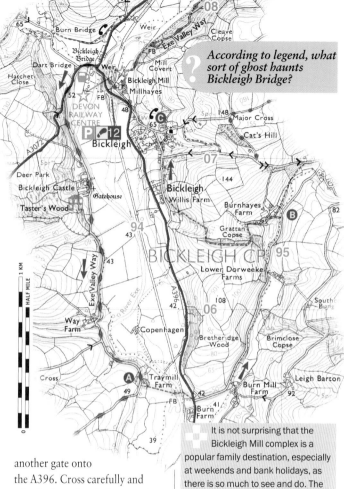

another gate onto the A396. Cross carefully and take the lane ahead, signposted to Butterleigh.

B After almost one mile (1.6km), turn left, at public footpath and Two Counties Way signs, and cross a bridge over a stream. Walk along a tarmac track, continue along a path between farm buildings, go

It is not surprising that the Bickleigh Mill complex is a popular family destination, especially at weekends and bank holidays, as there is so much to see and do. The mill has a **working water wheel**, plus shop and restaurant. Next to it the **Devon Railway Centre** is a haven for railway enthusiasts of all ages. The original Victorian railway station has been preserved and you can take rides both on a narrow gauge railway beside the River Exe and on a miniature railway, as well as enjoying the model train layouts.

through a gate and head uphill along a tree-lined, sunken track. On emerging into a field, turn left uphill along its left edge and look out for where you bear slightly left to continue uphill along an enclosed path through trees to a stile. Climb it, keep ahead and the route continues along the right edge of a field, by woodland on the right. Go through a gate, keep ahead and after about 100 yds (91m), look out for a right turn and climb up through trees to a stile. Climb it, keep ahead initially by the right field edge and then bear left and head across the field to a stile in the far corner. Climb it and continue steeply downhill across the next field to a gate by stables. Go through, walk in front of the stables, go through another gate and descend steps to a lane. Bear right along the narrow lane into Bickleigh village.

C At a T-junction, turn left downhill to the A396 again. Keep ahead, not along the road but along the tarmac drive to the right of it, and walk past Bickleigh Mill to return to the start. ●

> Bickleigh village and mill are on the east side of the Exe, the castle is on the west side. The **medieval castle** – more of a manor house – belonged to the Courtenay family, the Earls of Devon. Little is left apart from the large sandstone gatehouse. On the other side of the road is a **Norman chapel**. The village church dates mainly from the 13th century.

River Exe at Bickleigh

Budleigh Salterton and West Down

START Budleigh Salterton

DISTANCE 4 miles (6.4km)

TIME 2 hours

PARKING Budleigh Salterton

ROUTE FEATURES Easy, steady climbing along the Coast Path and field paths

13

From the centre of Budleigh Salterton, a steady climb over wooded cliffs brings you to the fine viewpoint of West Down Beacon, 423 ft (129m) high. A semi-circular walk across the down – much of it now occupied by a golf course – leads back to the Coast Path for the descent to the start.

The walk starts in front of the Fairlynch Museum. Facing it, turn right to the sea front and at a Coast Path sign, turn sharp right onto a tarmac path beside the stony beach. The path rises steadily and after going up steps, turn left in front of a door. Turn right, left again at a T-junction and then right again and where the tarmac path ends, keep ahead along the left edge of an open, grassy recreation area. Continue steadily uphill along an enclosed path over the cliffs, through gorse, bracken and trees, to West Down Beacon, the highest point.

Budleigh Salterton

Ⓐ At a waymarked post – just after the path starts to descend and by a triangulation pillar on the right – turn right along a path which winds across more gorse, bracken and trees on West Down.

PUBLIC TRANSPORT Buses from Exmouth and Sidmouth
REFRESHMENTS Pubs and cafés at Budleigh Salterton
PUBLIC TOILETS Budleigh Salterton
ORDNANCE SURVEY MAPS: Explorer 115 (Exmouth & Sidmouth), Landranger 192 (Exeter & Sidmouth)

Apart from a few old cottages, the resort of **Budleigh Salterton** is very much a creation of the 19th century. Handsome Victorian houses rise up from the long flat beach that extends from the mouth of the River Otter to the east to the cliffs on the west side and the town has a pleasantly old fashioned air. It gets its name from the salterns or salt pans in which sea water used to be evaporated. **The Fairlynch Museum**, housed in an early 19th-century thatched house – one of a number built in the area – is well worth a visit.

On emerging onto the corner of the East Devon golf course, bear slightly right away from its left edge to a footpath post and turn right between trees to a T-junction.

Turn left gently downhill along an enclosed track, later continuing along the left edge of the course, and where the track bears right, keep ahead along an enclosed path to a kissing-gate. Go through and walk across a field to a fingerpost on the far side.

B Turn right – the path is signposted Littleham Church Path – along the left field edge and go through a kissing-gate in the corner. Turn right across another small area of the golf course and then continue gently downhill along an enclosed path. Cross a track and keep ahead – later through woodland – to the B3178.

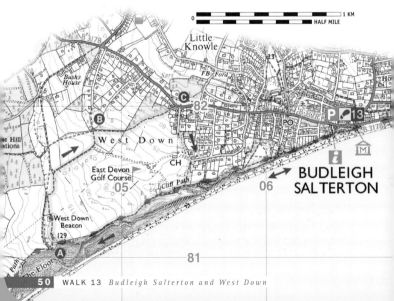

Cliffs near Budleigh Salterton

C Turn right and immediately turn right again along Links Road, heading uphill. Follow the road around left and right bends, pass to the left of the golf club car park and at the next left bend, turn right, at a public footpath sign, onto a path which curves left along the left edge of the course again to a footpath post. Keep ahead gently downhill through trees and bracken to a T-junction and turn left onto the Coast Path. Here you rejoin the outward route and retrace your steps to the start.

Which estuary can be seen from the path across West Down, just after leaving the Coast Path?

The superb views from **West Down Beacon** extend over much of East Devon and along the South Devon coast to the cliffs at Berry Head beyond Brixham. The granite tors of Dartmoor can be seen on the horizon and nearer at hand is the resort of Exmouth and the open heathlands of **Woodbury Common**.

14 Bigbury-on-Sea, Ringmore and Ayrmer Cove

START Bigbury-on-Sea
DISTANCE 4 miles (6.4km)
TIME 2 hours
PARKING Bigbury-on-Sea
ROUTE FEATURES Several ascents and descents – some quite steep – along tracks, field paths and the Coast Path

An undulating inland stretch across fields brings you to the picturesque village of Ringmore and from there an enclosed path leads to the coast at Ayrmer Cove. The last 1¼ miles (2km) is a superb roller-coaster walk along a dramatic section of the south Devon coast, with views ranging across Bigbury Bay to Bolt Tail and Wembury Head.

From the car park head up to the road and keep ahead uphill along Parker Road. Where the road ends, climb a stile and continue up over the brow of the hill along the right edge of three fields.

Ⓐ In the corner of the third field, turn left and head downhill along the right field edge to a gate. Go through and continue steeply downhill along the left edge of the next two fields to a track at the bottom. Bear left to a waymarked

Ayrmer Cove

PUBLIC TRANSPORT Occasional buses from Kingsbridge and Plymouth
REFRESHMENTS Pub at Ringmore, pub at Challaborough, beach cafés (seasonal) at Bigbury and Challaborough
PUBLIC TOILETS At start
ORDNANCE SURVEY MAPS Explorer OL 20 (South Devon), Landranger 202 (Torbay & South Dartmoor)

The small resort of Bigbury-on-Sea is superbly situated above a broad sandy bay opposite **Burgh Island**. The island is only cut off from the mainland for a short period and a stroll across the sands is the usual way of getting there but at high water an unusual and ingenious sea tractor is used. Burgh Island is chiefly noted for its large **Art Deco** hotel, built in the 1930s and visited by many of the wealthy celebrities of that era.

post, follow a path uphill across a field, climb a stile and descend steps to a lane. Go through the gate opposite, head downhill along the right edge of a field and in the corner, cross a footbridge over a brook and climb a stile. Walk uphill through a young plantation, go through a gate, continue up along an enclosed path and go through a kissing-gate onto a track. Turn

right, immediately turn left, go through a hedge gap and keep along the left edge of a field. After going through a kissing-gate in the corner, walk along a hedge-lined path to a tarmac track and keep ahead into the village of Ringmore. At a T-junction, turn right along a lane through the village.

B Turn left in front of the church and at a fork in front of the pub, take the left hand uphill lane. Turn right along a tarmac track and look out for where a public bridleway sign directs you to bear left along a tree-lined path to a gate. Go through and continue along an enclosed path which bends first to the right and then to the left and heads steadily downhill to Ayrmer Cove.

Bigbury-on-Sea and Burgh Island

C At a fingerpost, turn left onto the Coast Path and head steeply up over the cliffs. The path then descends to the beach at Challaborough, bending sharply left above the sands to emerge onto a track. Turn left to the road.

D Turn right alongside the beach and where the road bends left, keep ahead along an ascending path. Go through a gate, keep ahead to a road and walk down into Bigbury. At a Coast Path sign, bear slightly right down steps and the path leads back to the start. ●

> **?** Which famous writer of thrillers used to stay at the hotel on Burgh Island in the 1920s and 30s?

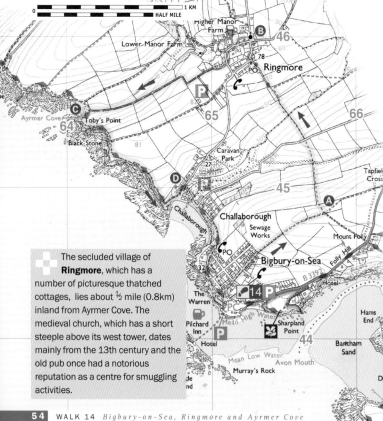

The secluded village of **Ringmore**, which has a number of picturesque thatched cottages, lies about ½ mile (0.8km) inland from Aymer Cove. The medieval church, which has a short steeple above its west tower, dates mainly from the 13th century and the old pub once had a notorious reputation as a centre for smuggling activities.

Walls Hill, Hope's Nose and Lincombe Woods

START Babbacombe, Walls Hill car park
DISTANCE 5 miles (8km)
TIME 3 hours
PARKING Walls Hill car park
ROUTE FEATURES Mainly along cliff top and woodland paths with small stretches of road walking, some moderate climbs

15

Despite being wholly within the built-up area of Torbay, this is a most attractive and unspoilt walk that embraces both splendid cliff top walking and some delightful woodland. It is an undulating route so expect several modest ascents and descents. From the Coast Path there are superb and extensive views over Tor Bay to Berry Head and across Babbacombe Bay towards Teignmouth.

Begin by taking the path that leads off from the far end of the car park, pass beside a barrier and continue across the downs to a Walls Hill noticeboard. Continue across it, over the grassy expanses of the hill and on reaching the cliff top, keep ahead along the Coast Path.

A Follow the cliff top as it curves right and at a Coast Path sign, continue along an enclosed path through woodland, turn left down steps, then turn right and head downhill – more steps in places – to a lane. Turn left and by Anstey's Cove car park, turn left beside a barrier, at a Coast Path sign, onto a path through more delightful woodland.

B The next stretch is called the Bishop's Walk. Follow an undulating path, pass beside a barrier and keep ahead along a tarmac drive which bends right to a road. Cross over and at a 'Coast

PUBLIC TRANSPORT Buses from Exeter, Teignmouth and Torquay
REFRESHMENTS Pubs and cafés at Babbacombe, café at Kent's Cavern
PUBLIC TOILETS Kent's Cavern
ORDNANCE SURVEY MAPS Explorer 110 (Torquay & Dawlish), Landranger 202 (Torbay & South Dartmoor)

Path, Hope's Nose' sign, turn left onto an uphill grassy path parallel to the road. The path becomes enclosed, curves right, continues up through trees and finally descends to a road.

C *For the detour to Hope's Nose, cross over, climb a stile and take the downhill path ahead. Go through a gate and continue on down to the end of the promontory.*

Retrace your steps to the road, turn left and follow the coast road around a right bend. On reaching an open grassy area dotted with bushes, trees and benches, turn left along its left edge and go through a hedge gap to Thatcher Point. Ahead is the prominent landmark of Thatcher Rock. Turn right along an enclosed path to rejoin the road.

D Turn left downhill and at a waymarked post about 100 yds (91m) before reaching a T-junction, turn left down steps, turn right down more steps, keep ahead across a car park and go up steps onto a road.

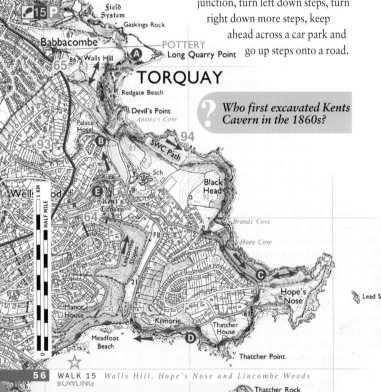

? *Who first excavated Kents Cavern in the 1860s?*

Tor Bay

At the time of publication, utility work was going on here and when completed, the route directions may be slightly different. However all paths will be clearly waymarked.

Cross the road, pass through a wall gap and barrier opposite and take the path ahead along the right edge of Lincombe Woods. At a fingerpost, turn left through a hedge gap, immediately turn right and continue by the right inside edge of the wood. Later the path bears left and heads uphill through the trees. Turn right at a fingerpost, in the Kent's Cavern direction, head first downhill, then climb steps and keep ahead to Kent's Cavern. Continue through the car park to a road.

E Turn right downhill and at a right bend, turn left – there is a public footpath sign to Anstey's Cove – along a tarmac path. Continue along the left edge of a field and on through Anstey's Cove car park to a lane. **B** Turn left, here rejoining the outward route, and retrace your steps to the start.

Kents Cavern has been attracting visitors for more than a century. The caves were first excavated in the 1860s and guided tours tell you about the prehistoric animals that used to roam here, the formation of the caves and how the Victorian explorers and archaeologists gradually uncovered their treasures and secrets. There is a visitor centre, shop and café.

● Attractive village ● estuary ● fine viewpoint ● spectacular coastline

16 *Shaldon and the Teign Estuary*

START Shaldon

DISTANCE 4½ miles (7.2km)

TIME 2½ hours

PARKING Shaldon, The Ness car park

ROUTE FEATURES Flat and easy walking beside the estuary is followed by several fairly steep climbs and descents along lanes, tracks and the Coast Path

The first part of the walk is mainly along tarmac paths beside the Teign estuary between Shaldon and Ringmore. You then turn inland for an 'up and down' stretch along narrow lanes, green roads and paths, passing the superb 554 ft (169m) high viewpoint of The Beacon. The final leg heads downhill along the Coast Path and over the wooded headland of The Ness, with dramatic views across the estuary to Teignmouth and beyond.

Turn left out of the car park and follow the lane through the attractive village. Where the lane bears left, keep ahead, passing to the right of a war memorial clock tower, and turn right at a crossroads. The lane curves left beside the Teign estuary to the main road by Teignmouth and Shaldon Bridge.

A Cross over and keep ahead along a tarmac track beside the estuary which curves left away from the river to a road. Turn right into Ringmore and the road bends left uphill through the village, passing to the left of the small 17th-century church. At a right bend, keep ahead along a lane (Higher Ringmore Road) which heads uphill between thatched cottages.

B About 200 yds (183m) beyond the last of the houses, turn right onto a hedge-lined track. The track winds uphill to a T-junction. Turn

PUBLIC TRANSPORT Buses from Exeter, Teignmouth and Torquay, ferry from Teignmouth

REFRESHMENTS Pubs and cafés at Shaldon

PUBLIC TOILETS Shaldon

ORDNANCE SURVEY MAPS Explorer 110 (Torquay & Dawlish), Landranger 192 (Exeter & Sidmouth)

right down a tarmac track to a lane, turn left uphill and on the brow of the hill, turn left again onto another hedge-lined track. This is a green road called Butterfly Lane and you follow it steadily uphill to emerge onto a lane at the viewpoint of The Beacon and a triangulation pillar.

C Turn left downhill and at a public footpath sign at the bottom, turn right over a stile. Head gently downhill along a fence-lined path which bears right to a stile. Climb it and keep ahead, over another stile and through a gate, to emerge onto the A379. Turn right and although you have to walk along it for only about 200 yds (183m), *take great care as it is a busy main road, there are no verges and it is quite narrow.*

D At the first bend, turn sharp left along a track to a stile – here joining the Coast Path – climb the stile and head downhill along the right edge of a field. Pass through a hedge gap and as you continue steeply down, there is a magnificent view ahead over Shaldon, the Teign estuary and Teignmouth. In the bottom corner of the field, go up steps to climb a stile, walk along an enclosed path, go through a hedge gap and continue along the right edge of a golf course. At the next corner, keep ahead through woodland and descend steps to a track. Turn right downhill and at a fork, take the right hand path through Ness Woodland. At the next fork, continue along the right hand path heading over the headland of The Ness to another superb viewpoint. Turn left, descend through the trees, by a wire fence on the right, go down steps and turn left alongside the shore to a lane. Turn left to return to the car park. ●

> **?** *In which year was the first wooden bridge built across the Teign estuary between Teignmouth and Shaldon?*

The Ness and Teignmouth

Bolt Tail and Bolberry Down

START Outer Hope, Hope Cove car park
DISTANCE 5 miles (8km)
TIME 2½ hours
PARKING Hope Cove car park
ROUTE FEATURES A fairly easy stretch of the Coast Path followed by lanes and tracks

Hope Cove is a particularly attractive settlement and there are beautiful and dramatic coastal views on the first part of the walk, especially across Bigbury Bay, as you follow the Coast Path through Hope Cove and around the headland of Bolt Tail before heading over the cliffs of Bolberry Down. The route then turns inland and follows mainly quiet, narrow lanes and tracks back to the start.

Turn left out of the car park through the picturesque hamlet of Outer Hope, passing to the left of the post office, and where the road ends, keep ahead along a tarmac path. Climb steps, keep ahead to emerge onto a lane and head downhill along it to a road in Inner Hope. Bear right and where the road bends left, keep ahead up a flight of steps. At the top the path bends right and continues to a kissing-gate. Go through, head steadily uphill through woodland to emerge onto open downland and continue up to the top of the

The ramparts of the Iron Age fort on **Bolt Tail** are still clearly visible and probably date from around 600BC. They were built across the neck of the peninsula to guard the fort from the landward side. Similar forts are to be found on many of Britain's coastal headlands.

headland of Bolt Tail, passing through the ramparts of a prehistoric fort. **Ⓐ** At a fork, take the left-hand path to a waymarked post and turn left. Continue along the south side of Bolt Tail and then follow a grassy path which is uphill, over the top of cliffs and

PUBLIC TRANSPORT Infrequent buses from Kingsbridge
REFRESHMENTS Pubs and cafés at Hope Cove, pub by Bolberry Down
PUBLIC TOILETS Hope Cove
ORDNANCE SURVEY MAPS Explorer OL20 (South Devon), Landranger 202 (Torbay & South Dartmoor)

descends slightly to a stile. Climb it, continue uphill, by a fence on the left, go through a gate at the top and continue across the open expanses of Bolberry Down. The path eventually bends left away from the cliffs and at a fork, take the left-hand path – here leaving the Coast Path – and continue along a tarmac path.

B Pass beside a barrier, turn right to a car park and turn left along a lane. Descend steeply to a T-junction, turn left and at a fork, take the right-hand narrow, winding lane downhill through the hamlet of Bolberry. The lane continues uphill.

C Where it bends right, keep ahead, at a footpath sign to Sweethearts Lane and Galmpton, along a narrow enclosed path. This may be overgrown at times. Descend to a T-junction, turn left along a track and at a public footpath sign to Galmpton and Hope Cove, turn right up steps and walk along an enclosed path to a stile. Climb it, head uphill across a field, climb another stile and turn right along a track.

D Immediately after going through a gate, turn left over a stone stile and walk along a track which keeps by the left edge of

Hope Cove from Bolt Tail

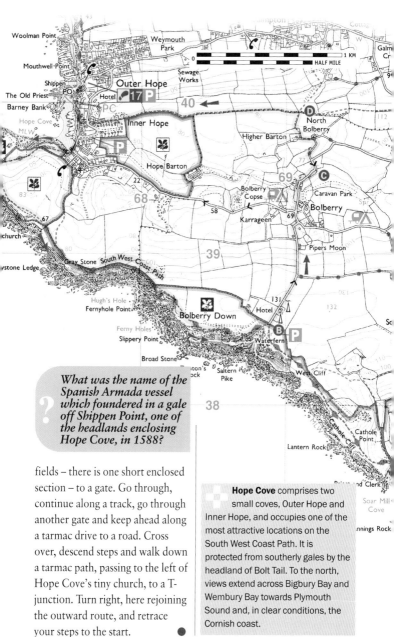

fields – there is one short enclosed section – to a gate. Go through, continue along a track, go through another gate and keep ahead along a tarmac drive to a road. Cross over, descend steps and walk down a tarmac path, passing to the left of Hope Cove's tiny church, to a T-junction. Turn right, here rejoining the outward route, and retrace your steps to the start. ●

Hope Cove comprises two small coves, Outer Hope and Inner Hope, and occupies one of the most attractive locations on the South West Coast Path. It is protected from southerly gales by the headland of Bolt Tail. To the north, views extend across Bigbury Bay and Wembury Bay towards Plymouth Sound and, in clear conditions, the Cornish coast.

18 *Ottery St Mary and the River Otter*

START Ottery St Mary

DISTANCE 5½ miles (8.9km)

TIME 3 hours

PARKING Ottery St Mary

ROUTE FEATURES Easy walking along tracks and field paths, much of it across riverside meadows

Apart from an opening stretch across fields, most of the walk is through woodland and across delightful meadows beside the River Otter. From many points there are fine views over the valley and both up and down the river. Historic interest is provided by the magnificent medieval church at Ottery St Mary.

The walk starts at the top of Silver Street in front of the church. Walk down Silver Street, curving left into The Square, turn left, passing the tourist information centre, and turn right along Tip Hill. On the brow of the hill, turn left along Longdogs Lane and head down to a crossroads.

A Turn right, at a public bridleway sign, along an enclosed tarmac track which becomes a hedge-lined path and reaches a gate. Go through, keep ahead along an enclosed track and at a fork by farm buildings, take the right hand lower track to a gate. Go through, continue down the track and bear right along a broader track, passing in front of a house (Knightstone). Cross a footbridge by a ford, go through gates onto a lane and turn right to a T-junction.

River Otter

PUBLIC TRANSPORT Buses from Sidmouth and Exeter

REFRESHMENTS Pubs and cafés at Ottery St Mary

PUBLIC TOILETS Ottery St Mary

ORDNANCE SURVEY MAPS Explorer 115 (Exmouth & Sidmouth), Landranger 192 (Exeter & Sidmouth)

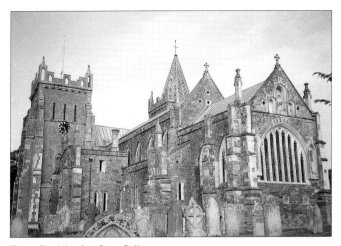

The medieval church at Ottery St Mary

B Turn right and almost immediately turn left through a gate, at a public footpath sign, and walk along a track by the bottom right edge of a sloping field. Go through a gate, keep ahead but at a footpath post before the next gate, bear left along a path to a stile. Climb it, walk along an enclosed path, turn left to climb steps up an embankment and continue along the top of the embankment. After climbing a stile, turn right along the right edge of a field, go through a gate and continue along an enclosed track which emerges into a field. Walk along its right edge, turn right over a stile in the corner, descend steps to climb another stile, descend more steps and bear left to continue by the River Otter.

Cross a footbridge, keep ahead through trees beside the river and climb a stile. Turn left up a track but almost immediately turn sharp right up to a stile. Climb it, walk along the right edge of a field, climb a stile and turn left up steps to climb another one. Turn right along the right edge of the next field, go through a gate, descend steps and continue through trees and bushes by the river again. Climb three more stiles and after going through a kissing-gate just after the third stile, climb a wooded embankment and continue along the right edge of the next field. Bear right to climb a stile in the corner, continue along a track, go through a gate and keep ahead by old mill buildings.

In the 18th century **Ottery St Mary** was an important wool centre and the town has a number of handsome Georgian buildings. The monument at the start of the walk, erected to commemorate Queen Victoria's Diamond Jubilee, is a copy of a gatepost at Kensington Palace. The poet **Samuel Taylor Coleridge**, was born here in 1772.

C Turn right to cross a footbridge over the river and turn right again. The return leg to Ottery St Mary is mainly along pleasant riverside meadows, keeping by the Otter most of the way and negotiating a series of stiles, footbridges and gates. The route is well-waymarked and there are just two places where you briefly leave the river to cut off a bend. Finally – shortly after passing a new Millennium Footbridge – climb a stile and ascend steps to a road.

D Turn right over a bridge and follow the road into Ottery St Mary. Where the main road bends left, keep ahead along Mill Street into The Square and turn left to return to the start. ●

? *On which famous building is the church at Ottery St Mary modelled?*

Meadows beside the Otter

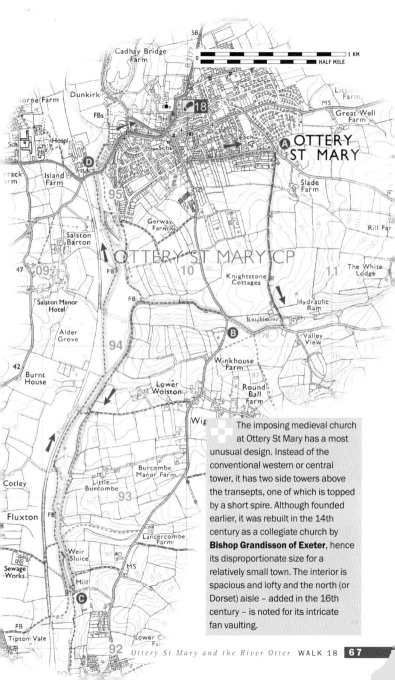

The imposing medieval church at Ottery St Mary has a most unusual design. Instead of the conventional western or central tower, it has two side towers above the transepts, one of which is topped by a short spire. Although founded earlier, it was rebuilt in the 14th century as a collegiate church by **Bishop Grandisson of Exeter**, hence its disproportionate size for a relatively small town. The interior is spacious and lofty and the north (or Dorset) aisle – added in the 16th century – is noted for its intricate fan vaulting.

19/9/วท   X

19 *Sidmouth and Ladram Bay*

START Sidmouth
DISTANCE 5½ miles (8.9km); shorter version 2½ miles (4km)
TIME 3 hours (1½ hours for shorter walk)
PARKING Sidmouth
ROUTE FEATURES Mostly along the Coast Path with two inland stretches, lots of cliff walking with two fairly steep climbs

The walk between Sidmouth and Ladram Bay provides continuously magnificent views, both inland over rolling countryside and in both directions along the coast. The highlight is the superb cliff scenery and interesting rock formations at Ladram Bay. The route is well-waymarked and easy to follow but fairly energetic.

The walk starts on the sea front at the corner of Fore Street and the Esplanade. Facing the sea, turn right and follow the road as it bears right uphill, later quite steeply. Where the road bears slightly right, keep ahead beside a gate, at a Coast Path sign, continue uphill along an enclosed tarmac path and pass beside another gate to rejoin the road.

A At a public footpath sign opposite a car park on the right, turn left through a kissing-gate and walk along the left edge of two fields. Before reaching the corner of the second field, bear right across to a waymarked post on the far side.

Near Sidmouth

PUBLIC TRANSPORT Buses from Exeter, Exmouth and Honiton
REFRESHMENTS Pubs and cafés at Sidmouth, pub at Ladram Bay
PUBLIC TOILETS Sidmouth
ORDNANCE SURVEY MAPS Explorer 115 (Exmouth & Sidmouth), Landranger 192 (Exeter & Sidmouth)

B *Turn left if doing the short walk*; for the full walk turn right – now on the Coast Path – to continue along the field edge. The path descends, via steps in places, to a kissing-gate. Go through, keep ahead along an enclosed path and go through another kissing-gate. Walk across a field, heading down into a dip and up again, go through a kissing-gate at a fingerpost and continue along the right inside edge of woodland.

C At the next fingerpost, keep ahead – here leaving the Coast Path – along a track which becomes hedge-lined and continues to a lane. Turn left and head gently downhill along an enclosed tarmac track – this is technically a public road. Follow it around a right bend to a T-junction and turn left to Ladram Bay.

D At a three-way fork, take the left hand tarmac path, here rejoining the Coast Path and keeping on it for the rest of the walk. The path curves left in front of the Three Rocks Inn and continues along the right edge of a play and picnic area to a kissing-gate. Go through, walk uphill

> As you walk westwards along the coast path from Sidmouth, the dramatic **red cliffs** at **Ladram Bay** soon come into view. Not only are the cliffs among the finest on the South Devon coast, but there are also a number of detached rock pillars, the home of thousands of sea birds.

Ladram Bay

along the right edge of a field, curving left and heading up to another kissing-gate in the corner. After going through that one, climb steps and continue over the wooded headland of High Peak to a T-junction. **C** Turn right – here temporarily rejoining the outward route – and retrace your steps as far as point **B** where you rejoin the shorter version of the walk. Keep ahead to a kissing-gate which admits you to the National Trust's Peak Hill property. Continue along a path which winds steeply downhill through woodland and along the cliff edge, finally descending steps to a road. Turn

right, here rejoining the outward route again, and retrace your steps down the road and along the promenade to the start. ●

Sidmouth, a resort noted for its gentility, occupies a sunny and sheltered position between steep sandstone cliffs at the mouth of the little River Sid. It became fashionable during, and just after, the Napoleonic Wars when the English aristocracy were cut off from their usual continental haunts and the town possesses a number of dignified Georgian and Regency villas. **Queen Victoria** stayed here as a young girl with her parents in 1819.

Cliffs near Sidmouth

The cliffs and stacks at Ladram Bay are composed of what kind of rock?

Rolling countryside near Sidmouth

20 Kingswear and the Dart Estuary

START Kingswear

DISTANCE 5½ miles (8.9km)

TIME 3 hours

PARKING Kingswear

ROUTE FEATURES Hilly tracks and an 'up and down' Coast Path, fairly strenuous

An opening ramble along the Coast Path above the well-wooded estuary of the River Dart is followed by an inland stretch, mainly along clear and well-surfaced tracks. The return follows a highly scenic but fairly strenuous section of the Coast Path. Both on the inland and coastal sections there is quite a lot of climbing but the views are outstanding, especially looking across the estuary to Dartmouth. Apart from the twin castles at Dartmouth and Kingswear, further historic interest is provided by the Daymark Tower and Brownstone Battery.

The wooded Dart estuary

🥾 Turn right out of the car park and walk along the road through Kingswear to the railway station. Where the road ends at the ferry, keep ahead under an arch and turn left up steps, at a Coast Path sign. At the top, turn right along a tarmac drive, heading steadily uphill, and the drive narrows to a path which emerges onto another drive. Walk along this winding, tree-shaded drive to where the Coast Path turns right.

PUBLIC TRANSPORT Buses from Brixham, ferries from Dartmouth

REFRESHMENTS Pubs and cafés at Kingswear

PUBLIC TOILETS Kingswear

ORDNANCE SURVEY MAPS Explorer OL20 (South Devon), Landranger 202 (Torbay & South Dartmoor)

Brownstone Battery

A Keep ahead along the drive, in the Brownstone direction, and at a fork, take the right-hand lower track. At a public footpath sign just in front of a house, turn right down a track and then continue steeply uphill along a stony path by the left inside edge of woodland. The path emerges onto a track and continue uphill along it, passing to the left of a farm.

B At a fingerpost, turn right, in the Coast Path direction, along a hedge-lined track. The track heads uphill and on meeting another track, bear right along it. Follow it around a right bend, pass to the right of the prominent Daymark

Tower – a stile and path give access to it – and head downhill towards the sea. Go through a kissing-gate to enter the National Trust's Froward Point property and continue downhill, passing through the Second World War defences of Brownstone Battery.

C Here you join the Coast Path and follow it, in the Kingswear direction, through woodland to a kissing-gate. Go through and then follows a steep and winding 'up and down' stretch to a stile. Climb it and as you continue through delightful woodland, grand views open up on the left of the Dart estuary and both Dartmouth and

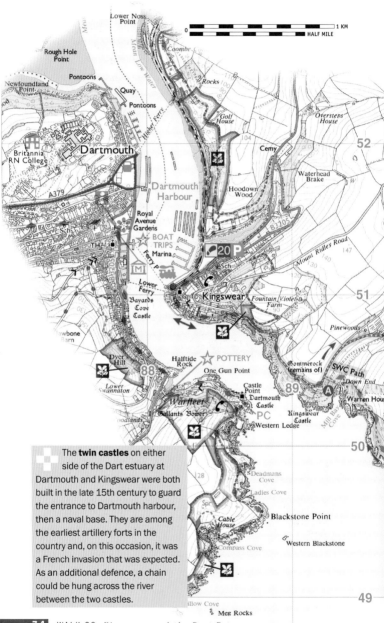

The **twin castles** on either side of the Dart estuary at Dartmouth and Kingswear were both built in the late 15th century to guard the entrance to Dartmouth harbour, then a naval base. They are among the earliest artillery forts in the country and, on this occasion, it was a French invasion that was expected. As an additional defence, a chain could be hung across the river between the two castles.

Kingswear castles. The path later bends right uphill, then goes left and descends steeply, via steps in places, to a tarmac track. Turn right and at a Coast Path sign, turn left along an enclosed path to a stile. Climb it, ascend a long flight of steps through woodland, cross a track and continue up more steps.

A At the top, turn left onto a tarmac drive, here rejoining the outward route, and retrace your steps to the start.

> **What was the purpose of the Daymark Tower?**

Above the Dart estuary

Further Information

Walking Safety

Always take with you both warm and waterproof clothing and sufficient food and drink. Wear suitable footwear, i.e. strong walking boots or shoes that give a good grip over stony ground, on slippery slopes and in muddy conditions. Try to obtain a local weather forecast and bear it in mind before you start. Do not be afraid to abandon your proposed route and return to your starting point in the event of a sudden and unexpected deterioration in the weather.

All the walks described in this book will be safe to do, given due care and respect, even during the winter. Indeed, a crisp, fine winter day often provides perfect walking conditions, with firm ground underfoot and a clarity of light unique to that time of the year.

The most difficult hazard likely to be encountered is mud, especially when walking along woodland and field paths, farm tracks and bridleways – the latter in particular can often get churned up by cyclists and horses. In summer, an additional difficulty may be narrow and overgrown paths, particularly along the edges of cultivated fields. Neither should constitute a major problem provided that the appropriate footwear is worn.

Follow the Country Code

- Enjoy the countryside and respect its life and work
- Guard against all risk of fire
- Take your litter home
- Fasten all gates
- Help to keep all water clean
- Keep your dogs under control
- Protect wildlife, plants and trees
- Keep to public paths across farmland
- Take special care on country roads
- Leave livestock, crops and machinery alone
- Make no unnecessary noise
- Use gates and stiles to cross fences, hedges and walls

(The Countryside Agency)

Useful Organisations

The Countryside Commission
John Dower House,
Crescent Place, Cheltenham,
Gloucestershire
GL50 3RA
Tel: 01242 521381

River Dart at Dittisham

The National Trust
Membership/general enquiries:
PO Box 39,
Bromley,
Kent
BR1 3XL
Tel: 0181 315 1111
(Devon Regional Office,
Killerton House, Broadclyst,
Exeter, Devon EX5 3LE
Tel: 01392 881691)

The Ramblers' Association
2nd Floor,
Camelford House,
87–89 Albert Embankment,
London
SE1 7TW.
Tel. 020 7339 8500

The Forestry Commission
Information Branch, 231
Corstorphine Road,
Edinburgh
EH12 7AT
Tel: 0131 334 0303

The Youth Hostels Association
Trevelyan House,
Dimple Road, Matlock,
Derbyshire
DE4 3YH.
Tel. 01629 592600

**Long Distance Walkers'
Association**
Bank House, High Street,
Wrotham, Sevenoaks,
Kent TN15 7AE.
Tel. 01732 883705

The Council for the Protection of Rural England
128 Southwark Street,
London SE1 0SW
Tel. 020 7981 2800

Ordnance Survey
Romsey Road, Maybush,
Southampton SO16 4GU
Tel: 08456 05 05 05 (Lo-call)

Local Organisations
Devon County Council
County Hall,
Lucombe House, Topsham Road,
Exeter EX2 4QW
Tel: 01392 382000

South Devon AONB Unit,
Coast and Countryside Service,
Follaton House, Plymouth Road,
Totnes, Devon TQ9 5NE
Tel: 01803 861140

Local Tourist Information Centres
West Country Tourist Board
60 St David's Hill, Exeter EX4 4SY
Tel: 01392 276351
Local Tourist Information offices:
Axminster: 01297 34386
Bodmin: 01208 76616
Brixham: 0906 680 1268
Budleigh Salterton: 01395 445275
Crediton: 01363 772006

Teign estuary near Shaldon

Start Point

Dartmouth: 01803 834224
Exeter: 01392 265700
Honiton: 01404 43716
Launceston: 01566 772321/772333
Lyme Regis: 01297 442138
Newton Abbot: 01626 215667
Okehampton: 01837 53020
Ottery St Mary: 01404 813964
Plymouth: 01752 304849
Salcombe: 01548 843927
Sidmouth: 01395 516441
Torquay: 01803 297428
Totnes: 01803 863168

Public Transport
For all public transport enquiries:
Traveline: 0870 608 2 608

Ordnance Survey Maps
The walks described in this guide
are covered by Ordnance Survey
1:50,000 scale (1¼ inches to 1 mile
or 2cm to 1km) Landranger map
sheets 191, 192, 201, 202. These
all-purpose maps are packed with
information to help you explore
the area. Viewpoints, picnic sites,
places of interest and caravan and
camping sites are shown, as well as
public rights of way information
such as footpaths and bridleways.

To examine the area in more
detail, and especially if you are
planning walks, the Ordnance
Survey Explorer maps at 1:25 000
scale (2½ inches to 1 mile or 4cm

to 1km) are ideal. Maps covering the area are:

OL20 (South Devon)
OL28 (Dartmoor)
110 (Torquay & Dawlish)
114 (Exeter & the Exe Valley)
115 (Exmouth & Sidmouth)
116 (Lyme Regis & Bridport)

To get to South Devon and Dartmoor use the Ordnance Survey Great Britain Routeplanner (Travelmaster map number 1).

Ordnance Survey maps and guides are available from most booksellers, stationers and newsagents.

Answers to Questions

Walk 1: Any two of these – London Bridge, British Museum, National Gallery.
Walk 2: Exmouth.
Walk 3: It is Parliament Street, almost opposite where you join High Street, 25 inches wide at first and gradually widening to 45 inches.
Walk 4: Trinity House.
Walk 5: To the local people of Slapton and other villages in the South Hams – for giving up their homes to aid the war effort in the Second World War.
Walk 6: Between 500 and 300BC.
Walk 7: Because it was almost destroyed in an air raid in 1943.
Walk 8: Ralph de Pomeroy, a supporter of William the Conqueror.
Walk 9: 18 ft (5.5m)
Walk 10: Charles II.
Walk 11: May 19, 1984.
Walk 12: A headless knight. He had his head cut off while fighting with another knight on the bridge.
Walk 13: The estuary of the River Exe.
Walk 14: Agatha Christie.
Walk 15: William Pengelly.
Walk 16: 1827.
Walk 17: San Pedro el Major.
Walk 18: Exeter Cathedral.
Walk 19: Sandstone.
Walk 20: It was built as an aid to navigation along the South Devon coast and is still in use today.

Bickleigh Castle